Gulab jamun

Jana Tayfour

BookLeaf Publishing

Presentation by *BookLeaf Publishing*

Web: www.bookleafpub.com

E-mail: info@bookleafpub.com

ISBN: 9789357213523

First edition 2023

Vernada

Each one of us is born to deliver a message; with every child born, a light shines in the diamond sky, this light carries a song that will be carved on this Newborn's heart. Ancestors believed that our destinies are where the lights meet, but what did they mean by that? What's in a light that can draw our destinies? The ancestors always know where the light goes; they talked about a polar realm, where all the lights intersect together; the mother light and the reflection of our dreams and hopes.

light

Vernada! Legends say that a light was born from the seventh skies, the sea; the mighty perfidious sea would shiver when this light reflects on its clear surface that it exploded. Millions are waiting for it; this light they said is so powerful that you might fall for it at the first sight.

she stood there

She stood there facing the moon, the moonlight reflected on her face. Her face was so bright like the twinkling diamonds in the starry black sky. Vernada was always so bright and so beautiful; they say that a shooting star created her which made her so bright. She shone like drop of rain meeting the earliest ray of summer. This time she was pale white like a ghost without a soul. She was gazing forward to the moon .She looked so distressed, her eyes; I saw them carrying the misery of thousand years.

running

I ran and ran, I called her, but she seemed that she never heard me at all nor turned to me. “Vernada, I called “Vernada”. I called until my voice faded into space. I stood there, gazing at her devastatingly with crystals running down my eyes...Hear me Vernada; you are my music. Suddenly; I saw her fade little by little, she was now a mirage glowing.

maiden

The course of life…The years that built us... The days we felt like burying ourselves to death... The days that made us believe we can touch the sun. We always had markers in our memory that shaped how we feel and sense. This memory in this is so old...It's about a Maiden... The maiden that sends wonderful memories to us to forget the bad ones. She was a maiden. She was beautiful, delicate like a rose petal. Shiny like sun reflecting on a pure white crystal. She is never seen, but always felt in memories. She sends and receives by summoning waves in the sea.

you and me

Over those misty landscapes
Through those mighty rivers
Somewhere near the mountains
Where man never went
Where the sun sets in the horizon
Where it rises with glory
Where lavenders are blooming
Where daffodils are swarming
Up where the soul is breathing
The elixir of purity and devotion
Purity of heart that swore to be faithful
Devotion to a better half and companion
We overlooked the scenery
Who knows ?
Who knows the days ahead
Except for the creator of this masterpiece
What can it hide in its folds
That we are still bound to know
What pictures our eyes will click
When faced with certain emotions

together

My eyes only see this moment now
Here where the sea sets
Here where my world starts and ends
For now I only see this scene
As if it was yesterday
Yesterday that my soul was reborn
When I knew our hearts will beat as one
Even if I don't know what the world hides
I have my world with me
In every step I take and wherever I go
Keep gazing with me
This is how I feel secure
Let me meditate and reflect
For when I go back
Let me remember the love I felt
When you and me saw this scene for the first
time

Kindred spirits

Two pearls born in the ocean depth
as rare as gold
Who wins them is sure to be blessed
or so I was told
I dived deep to the ocean
to their secret worth discovery
they are lanterns glowing with pure love
if in your heart they stay
with a single heartbeat
your life will be forever changed

pearls

I knew from there
that is was a matter of fate
and that my life with those pearls
is a treasure for me to keep
little did I know about them
but now that I know
My life with them is full of love , freedom and blessings
Brining out allah's best gifts in me
expecting of nothing in return
My smile is forever glowing
their love in me is blooming
love them all heart and all
because they are my pearls
my pearls from the deep ocean

Me

I'm a fictional character
a reader and a dreamer
I'm free-spirited like Joe
I'm determined like Anne
I feel sophisticated like Amy
I enjoy dancing in balls
I enjoy writing and making calls
I surround myself with Kindred spirits
and my soul never grows old

If I were a book

If I were a book
I will write my own story
my characters will be unique
their lives are intertwined
in their hearts they always seek
they seek love , care and warmth
they aren't always right
or always wrong
they make mistakes
but they try to repent
they take risks
but they reach their goals
If I were a book, the world will be my stage
I will give everyone life
and make the reader not dare look away
if I can make the reader my friend
I will be happy and blessed

my smile

My smile is forever glowing
their love in me is blooming
love them all heart and all
because they are my pearls
my pearls from the deep ocean

I'm an artist

I'm an artist
I paint my world
I paint my house of dreams
The dreams that are happy and sad
my toys scattered all around
I fly into the sky
I burn to a free bird
embracing life
embracing my existence

Love

What is love
I always ask
is it what I seek
is it just a dream
It's a mystery for me
a mystery for eternity
how can two souls
different like the sun and moon
connect and become kindred spirits
Maybe one day I will feel the same
when I meet my kindred spirit one day

I'm tough

I'm tough
I'm strong
I'm afraid sometimes
but a coward never
I know I make mistakes
but regrets I have none
My own path I carved on my own
with the help of loved ones in my life
I know no fear
I know no limits
I'm tough
I'm strong

I'm a reader

I'm a reader
I travel in each book I read
Today I'm a detective solving an impossible case
Now I'm a teacher , a lady of superior grace
Later I'm travelling on a ship
crossing the blue sea
I can be a scientist
discovering something new
or I could be fairy
flying to the rescue
why not a knight
saving someone beautiful
or perhaps a spy for a king
a guard for a princess
a guardian of a galaxy
I'm a reader , so I live all those lives
I live them daily
They live in me
they share my stories and I share theirs
I'm a reader
I travel for free

To me

I wrote a letter for myself
when I was a little girl
I wrote to myself
a letter full of love
for a little girl that's growing
Grow little girl
go explore and see the world
there are hidden gates
to a future faraway
don't try to figure it all out
for life has surprises
in every corner there is a door
taking you everywhere
Spread your wings
Fly away
write about what you see
what you feel and hear
embrace yourself
and enjoy your life
one day you will be happy
but also remember that it's okay to cry tears
at times you will feel confused
but remember that your heart is your guide
you will feel loved
but get ready to feel hatred

but inside stay pure
Keep the sparkle inside you
keep your spirit young
wear your heart on your sleeve
take a breath and live
for one day you will reach your destination
and fulfill your dreams

growing up

I grew up
I think it was so fast
My timeline flew by
a movie in my mind
I close my eyes to recall
a child long ago
who longed to grow
to explore and and fly
she has always tried
to face her fears
to reach her dreams
She laughed
she cried
she loved
she dreamed
she is now a young lady
still drinking the elixir of life
still learning to be brave
but her heart is like a lion's
brave, loyal and true
her spirit like a pheonix
burning like a fire that never goes off
she cried
she laughed
she know she isn't perfect

but she also knew
that her future is still calling
her heart is still alive

a box of chocolate

a box of chocolate
full of flavour
vanilla, caramel and custard flavour
a box of chocolate
wrapped with a red ribbon
when I'm alone
I untie the ribbon
I sit on my comfy chair
my hands ruffle through my hair
I think of my chocolate choice
what do I feel like tonight
caramel chocolate so dream
or dark chocolate so classy
do I go for something daring
like white raspberry chocolate so fancy?
what is it in this box of chocolate
what flavour in it I will find
My heart beats and my smile I feel
whenever I get a chocolate box
full of chocolate fancies

moonlight

I swear loyalty to thee- moonlight
Here by the moonlight
I lean against my window sill
Here with the depth of night
I think of thee face in the moonlight
I see you ,, I feel you ,, by moonlight
Dear,, if my love to you was a universe
then the world would feel limitless
if my love is a moon sky
then my moon shall wish you goodnight
my stars will illuminate your dreams
If my love was in words
(as if my love can be expressed by words)
lets say an ocean with no shores
a river with no banks
I LOVE U
I swear loyalty to thee
even if I need a bridge of light to reach you
even when my skies are grey
you will be my row of yellow daffodils
if my eyes can't see but darkness
your eyes are my moon lantern
I still swear loyalty to thee
even if waves kept crashing on my moon shores
I see you calling me

I count the steps that takes me back home
to you
to your moonlight
my moonlight is somewhat dim
for your moonlight is the source
of my existence
I shall wait for thee by moonlight

I love you

love your words and silence
I love your happiness and sadness
I love your soul and heart and all
I love you inside out and more
I love everything about you ❤
Love you ● and miss you

www.ingramcontent.com/pod-product-compliance
Lightning Source LLC
Chambersburg PA
CBHW051720130826
49812CB00034B/1267
* 9 7 8 9 3 5 7 2 1 3 5 2 3 *